IMAGES OF
THE FALL OF BERLIN

RARE PHOTOGRAPHS FROM WARTIME ARCHIVES

Ian Baxter

Pen & Sword
MILITARY

First published in Great Britain in 2019 by
PEN & SWORD MILITARY
An imprint of
Pen & Sword Books Ltd
47 Church Street
Barnsley
South Yorkshire
S70 2AS

ISBN 978-1-52673-787-8

Typeset by Concept, Huddersfield, West Yorkshire HD4 5JL
Printed and bound in India by Replika Press Pvt. Ltd

Pen & Sword Books Limited incorporates the imprints of Atlas, Archaeology, Aviation, Discovery, Family History, Fiction, History, Maritime, Military, Military Classics, Politics, Select, Transport, True Crime, Air World, Frontline Publishing, Leo Cooper, Remember When, Seaforth Publishing, The Praetorian Press, Wharncliffe Local History, Wharncliffe Transport, Wharncliffe True Crime and White Owl.

For a complete list of Pen & Sword titles please contact
PEN & SWORD BOOKS LIMITED
47 Church Street, Barnsley, South Yorkshire S70 2AS, England
E-mail: enquiries@pen-and-sword.co.uk
Website: www.pen-and-sword.co.uk

Contents

About the Author

Ian Baxter is a military historian who specialises in German twentieth-century military history. He has written more than fifty books including *Poland – The Eighteen Day Victory March*, *Panzers In North Africa*, *The Ardennes Offensive*, *The Western Campaign*, *The 12th SS Panzer-Division Hitlerjugend*, *The Waffen-SS on the Western Front*, *The Waffen-SS on the Eastern Front*, *The Red Army at Stalingrad*, *Elite German Forces of World War II*, *Armoured Warfare*, *German Tanks of War*, *Blitzkrieg*, *Panzer-Divisions at War*, *Hitler's Panzers*, *German Armoured Vehicles of World War Two*, *Last Two Years of the Waffen-SS at War*, *German Soldier Uniforms and Insignia*, *German Guns of the Third Reich*, *Defeat to Retreat: The Last Years of the German Army At War 1943–45*, *Operation Bagration – the Destruction of Army Group Centre*, *German Guns of the Third Reich*, *Rommel and the Afrika Korps*, *U-Boat War*, and most recently *The Sixth Army and the Road to Stalingrad*. He has written over a hundred articles including 'Last days of Hitler', 'Wolf's Lair', 'The Story of the V1 and V2 Rocket Programme', 'Secret Aircraft of World War Two', 'Rommel at Tobruk', 'Hitler's War With his Generals', 'Secret British Plans to Assassinate Hitler', 'The SS at Arnhem', 'Hitlerjugend', 'Battle of Caen 1944', 'Gebirgsjäger at War', 'Panzer Crews', 'Hitlerjugend Guerrillas', 'Last Battles in the East', 'The Battle of Berlin', and many more. He has also reviewed numerous military studies for publication, supplied thousands of photographs and important documents to various publishers and film production companies worldwide, and lectures to various schools, colleges and universities throughout the United Kingdom and the Republic of Ireland.

Introduction

Drawing on a superb collection of rare and unpublished photographs, this latest book in the popular Images of War Series provides a captivating insight into the fall of Berlin. In dramatic detail it analyses the German defence in front of the Reich capital and then its final collapse. Accompanied by in-depth captions and text, the book shows how Wehrmacht, Waffen-SS, Luftwaffe, Hitlerjugend, and Volkssturm personnel struggle to defend every yard of ground against an overwhelming enemy.

A German PaK gun positioned in the snow during a lull in the fighting in January 1945. This photograph was taken just before the great Russian winter offensive. The assault was to be a massive two-pronged attack through Poland, one leading along the Warsaw–Berlin axis commanded by Zhukov, the other for Breslau under the command of General Konev. The main objective was the Reich and Berlin.

(**Above**) Inside a Polish town and German PaK gunners wearing their winter whites are seen during a defensive action. The Germans contested every town and village as they were forced to withdraw westwards.

(**Opposite, above**) Clad in their winter whites these German troops are seen keeping low along a snowy embankment. The Red Army offensive was initiated on 12 January 1945, and two days later Zhukov's 1st Byelorussian Front began its long awaited drive along the Warsaw–Berlin axis, striking out from the Vistula south of Warsaw. The city was quickly encircled and fell three days later. The frozen ground ensured rapid movement for the Russian tanks.

(**Opposite, below**) Grenadiers armed with the Panzerfaust can be seen before an operation. During the last year of the war the Panzerfaust was used extensively to combat Russian armour. It was a handheld rocket-propelled grenade, effective at a range of about 200 feet.

(**Opposite, above**) A whitewashed StuG III Ausf G during a winter operation supporting grenadiers. In spite of the StuGs' proven value on the battlefield both in offensive and defensive roles, their increasing use as anti-tank weapons deprived the infantry of the fire support for which the assault gun was originally built. By early 1945, many StuGs were lost as a result.

(**Opposite, below**) An interesting photograph showing a StuG III Ausf G during an operation with infantry hitching a lift. To maintain their speed, the accompanying infantry were often carried on the tanks and other armoured vehicles. When they ran into opposition, they immediately dismounted to avoid taking casualties.

(**Above**) In a defensive position an 8.8cm flak gun can be seen being readied for a fire mission. Its gun barrel is in a horizontal position scanning the area for possible ground targets. In some sectors of the front, some units barely had enough tanks to oppose Russian armour and called upon flak battalions to halt the Red Army's attacks. During this later period many flak guns came to be assigned dual purposes, adding an anti-tank role to their operational duties.

(**Opposite, above**) An interesting photograph showing a whitewashed 8.8cm flak gun defensive position complete with Schützchild (splinter shield). Its gun barrel is trained in a horizontal position against possible ground targets.

(**Opposite, below**) German troops pose along the front standing next to one of their defensive positions. Along miles of the defensive front German divisions comprised handfuls of anti-tank and artillery guns strung out along the lines interspersed by a few bunkers, concrete defensive positions and anti-tank trenches.

(**Above**) A 10.5cm le FH 18/42 infantry gun crew in action. Throughout the war the 10.5cm gun provided both regular and Waffen-SS troops with a versatile, relatively mobile, base of fire.

(**Opposite, above**) A PaK crew during a defensive operation. During the Russian winter offensive German units were continually falling back from one defence line to another, trying desperately to keep the Red Army from bursting through into Germany and on to Berlin.

(**Opposite, below**) Tank crews are seen conversing. Along whole areas of the front the once-proud Panzer divisions had been reduced to skeletal formations on a stricken field. They were now not only vastly outnumbered but seriously lacked fuel supplies, lubricants and ammunition. When parts of the front caved in, armoured formations were often forced to destroy their equipment so nothing was left for the conquering enemy. The Germans no longer had the manpower, war plant or transportation to accomplish a proper build-up of forces on the Oder. Commanders could do little to compensate for the deficiencies, and in many sectors of the front they did not have any coherent planning in the event that the defence of the river failed.

(**Above**) A Russian tank column halted in the snow in February 1945. The Soviet First Byelorussian and First Ukrainian Fronts had the Germans outnumbered 10:1 in tanks and 9:1 in artillery and troops. The First Byelorussian Front alone had more infantry, tanks and artillery than the entire German army on the Eastern Front.

Russian anti-tank gunners seen with their Model 1932 L/46. The Model 1932 remained in service throughout the war. It was based on the German 3.7cm PaK35/36 anti-tank gun.

Three photographs taken in sequence showing a line of Soviet 76.2mm field guns trained on German positions during the winter thaw in March 1945. The gun had a range of 14,000 yards and, like most Russian guns of this generation, an anti-tank capability with solid shot.

(**Above**) A photograph of Hitler making a visit to his front line troops. Hitler made a brief tour of the front near the Oder in early March 1945 while visiting General Busse's 9th Army headquarters for a conference. This was the last time he would visit a combat zone. Only a month earlier German forces in the east had been driven back to the River Oder, the last bastion of defence before Berlin. Three weeks earlier, the Eastern Front was still deep in Poland. Now Upper Silesia was lost; in East Prussia German forces were smashed to pieces; West Prussia and Pomerania were being defended by depleted troops thrown together, and the defence of the Oder was now being entrusted to exhausted armies that had been fighting defensive actions for months in Poland along the Vistula. What was left of these forces were supposed to hold the Oder front and fight to the death.

(**Opposite**) Panzergrenadiers rest inside a shallow ditch in a field during a withdrawal operation on the Eastern Front. In the distance a column of armoured and support vehicles can be seen moving along a road.

A Nashorn tank destroyer advances along a road. Its potent 8.8cm PaK43 dual anti-tank/anti-aircraft gun tube can be seen protected to prevent dust, dirt particles and moisture entering the barrel during its drive. The Nashorn, although not so common by early 1945, still proved to be a highly effective tank killer. It was replaced in late 1944 by the Jagdpanzer IV and Jagdpanther.

Chapter One

Vistula-Oder Offensive

On 12 January 1945, the Soviet winter offensive was finally mobilised against the weakening German front in Poland. Konev's offensive began with the 1st Ukrainian Front making deep wide-sweeping penetrations against hard-pressed German formations. On the first day the 4th Panzer Army took the full brunt of an artillery barrage followed by an armoured attack by the 1st Byelorussian Front. The following day the second East Prussian Offensive was launched.

The main drive of the offensive pierced through the heart of Poland westwards towards the Warsaw–Berlin axis, striking out from the Vistula River south of Warsaw. Within days Krakov was encircled and fell three days later on 17 January. The frozen ground ensured rapid movement for the Russian tank crews, but in some areas these advances were halted for a time by the skilful dispositions of Panzers, supporting troops, and defensive lines comprising mazes of intricate blockhouses and trenches. Towns that fell in the path of these defensive belts were evacuated. Thousands of women, children and old men were pressed into service to help construct anti-tank trenches and other obstacles.

While it appeared that the Germans were well defended, much of the equipment employed along the defensive belts was too thinly spread. To make matters worse, the Russians began bombing German positions along the frontier.

In spite of this, the Russians were met by very strong resistance in several areas. However, German forces continued to fall back, and were well aware that they needed to prevent the Red Army from crossing the borders of the Reich and onto the River Oder, which was no more than 50 miles from the Reich capital, Berlin.

By the end of January 1945 the Soviets had captured Warsaw, Lodz, Krakow and Poznan, and were driving the German forces west. Only three weeks earlier, the Eastern Front was still deep in Poland. Now Upper Silesia was lost and in East Prussia German forces were fighting for survival. Königsberg and Kolberg were involved in bitter defences, while Danzig braced itself for the last battle. Elsewhere on the Baltic coast, isolated areas of German resistance fought on, but they had no real prospect of holding back the Red Army. Hitler had made it clear that Army Group Kurland was not to be evacuated. Every soldier, he said, was to stand and fight. What Hitler had done in one sentence was to condemn to death some 8,000 officers and 180,000 soldiers and Luftwaffe personnel. Some did escape the destruction of Army Group Kurland and retreated back towards the Oder or returned by ship to Germany.

While German units in the north fought to hold onto their positions and prevent the Baltic States from collapsing, further south the situation for Army Group A was just as dire. Army Group A comprised three armies: 9th, 4th Panzer, and the 17th. The group comprised some 450,000 soldiers, 4,000 artillery pieces, and 1,150 tanks. It was initially led by Colonel General Josef Harpe who was later disgraced following his withdrawal through Poland. He was replaced on 20 January by Colonel General Ferdinand Schörner. Schörner was under no illusion about the seriousness of the situation. German intelligence had estimated that the Russians had a 3:1 numerical superiority; there was in fact a 5:1 superiority.

To avoid what Hitler referred to as the complete extinction of Army Group A, Army Group Vistula was created on 24 January 1945. The new group was intended to protect Berlin from Soviet armies advancing from the Vistula River. It was formed from an assortment of rebuilt, new and existing units and Hitler decided that Heinrich Himmler would take control of it. Although Army Group Vistula were poorly matched in terms of equipment and supply against the Red Army, many of the troops were hardened veterans who had survived some of the hardest battles in the East.

But still the Russians advanced. The Soviet 4th Tank Army was reported to have reached the Oder and secured a bridgehead at Steinau. A week later, on 31 January, it voluntarily halted. Although the Russians were aware that Berlin was virtually un-defended and less than 50 miles away, orders had been sent to the various com-mands to consolidate positions before resuming their march on the Reich capital.

While the Soviets carried out mopping up operations against German defensive positions, it soon became apparent that Himmler lacked proper experience as a military commander, as much of the front he was commanding was collapsing at a far greater rate than at first anticipated. In an effort to stabilise the situation, Himmler was replaced by General Gotthard Heinrici as commander on 20 March. Troops and armoured vehicles were positioned along the main roads and highways, others were scattered in towns and villages, while heavy machine gun platoons dug in and held each end of the line. Crude obstacles were erected and troops were emplaced in defensive positions armed with a motley assortment of anti-tank and flak guns, machine guns, Panzerfaust and Panzerschreck.

For the Russians the Vistula-Oder Offensive was a major success. In a matter of days the Soviets had advanced hundreds of miles, sweeping away German positions, taking the bulk of Poland and striking deep across the previous borders of the Reich. The offensive had effectively smashed and dismembered Army Group A, and much of Germany's capacity to resist. While stubborn resistance continued to rage in Silesia, Pomerania and East Prussia, the Russians had time to prepare for the final offensive towards Berlin. The Wehrmacht also had time to build up forces between the Oder and in front of Berlin.

Russian anti-tank gunners on a road with their Model 1932 L/46 anti-tank gun. A troop leader raises his arm to signal his men to halt.

On the advance and a Russian Maxim 10 machine gun crew can be seen hauling their weapon across a field towards the battlefront. A mortar crew can also be seen preparing for action. It is possible that this photograph may have been staged.

Russian tanks halted on a road bound for the Oder in the early spring of 1945. Along the Oder the Germans no longer had the manpower, war plant or transportation to accomplish a proper build-up of forces. German commanders could do little to compensate for the deficiencies, and in many sectors of the front they did not have any coherent planning in the event the defence of the river failed.

Red Army troops seen in a long column of horse-drawn transport moving towards the front.

A Soviet T-34 tank hurtles along a dusty road during an operation. The T-34 was the mainstay of the Red Army armoured force. Although its design would be modified and refined to meet the ever increasing firepower of the Panzer, it would eventually see some 80,000 being produced during World War Two, which the Panzerwaffe could not match.

An 8.8cm flak gun is being limbered up following a fire mission against an enemy ground target. The gun's limber was always positioned nearby for the crew to rapidly limber up and reposition the gun.

Waffen-SS and regular troops inside a defensive position during Army Group Vistula operations. As the Russians advanced soldiers were ordered to erect crude obstacles and troops were emplaced in defensive positions armed with a motley assortment of anti-tank and flak guns, machine guns, Panzerfaust and Panzerschreck.

Russian soldiers seen smiling as they converse inside a forest clearing during a lull in their advance towards the Oder. Some are armed with the PPAh-1941 sub-machine gun.

An interesting photograph showing the crew of a Panzerwerfer 42 Maultier halftrack loading projectiles into its Nebelwerfer 42 launching system. The Nebelwerfer 42 consisted of ten gun tubes with the crew carrying some twenty projectiles, enough to fire two full salvos.

A knocked-out Jagdpanzer IV on the side of a road. With the drastic need for new armoured fighting vehicles more second generation tank destroyers were built. One such vehicle that came off the production line in 1944 was the Jagdpanzer IV. This vehicle, built on the chassis of a Pz.Kpfw.IV, weighed 28.5 tons and was nicknamed 'Guderian Duck'. It was the equal of any enemy tank thanks to its potent 7.5cm gun. The Jagdpanzer saw extensive service in the east and with its reliability and well sloped thick frontal armour it became a highly efficient fighting vehicle, if only for a short period of time.

A Panther tank has been knocked out of action. Everywhere it seemed the Germans were being forced to retreat. Scattered units fought bloody defences. Panzers tried their best to support them, but there were too few to make a decisive difference.

Two photographs taken in sequence showing a knocked-out Tiger tank on a road somewhere east of Berlin in spring 1945. By this late period of the war the Panzerwaffe did not have enough tanks to stem the tide of the mighty Red Army, but even so courageous Tiger crews fought valiantly on to prolong the death throes of its force.

(**Opposite, above**) During their retreat to the Oder, German troops can be seen conversing at a railway hub in Kustrin. Air raids destroyed the railway hub and almost all the surrounding buildings during the German withdrawal from the area east of the Oder during the Oder-Neisse operation. On 11 March 1945 Kustrin was captured by the Soviets.

(**Opposite, below**) A flak gun being positioned on a road during a defensive operation inside a town. The surrounding buildings all lay deserted and appear to have seen bitter fighting. A burned-out support vehicle can also be seen on the road.

(**Above**) An Sd.kfz.251 halftrack can be seen on a road moving at speed. Behind it in the distance are other vehicles including a motorcycle. By this period of the war the Sd.Kfz.251 had become not just a halftrack intended to simply transport infantry to the edge of the battlefield, but also a fully-fledged fighting vehicle.

(**Opposite, above**) On the move is an Sd.kfz.251/17 which can clearly be seen mounting an anti-aircraft vehicle armed with a 2cm KwK 38 attached on a pedestal with a small armoured turret to protect the gunner. Late in the war, these were issued as a platoon commander's vehicle to replace the Sd.Kfz.251/10.

(**Opposite, below**) A column of Russian IS-2 tanks bound for the front in March 1945. These tanks were designed with thick armour to counter the German 8.8cm guns. The IS-2 were mainly designed as breakthrough tanks, firing heavy high-explosive shells against German defensive positions such as bunkers. The tank went into service in April 1944 and was used to spearhead its armoured columns in the final stage of the battle of Berlin.

(**Above**) A Volkssturm armed with the lethal Panzerschreck or tank destroyer. It was known to the troops as the RPzB – the Raketenpanzerbuchse, or rocket tank rifle. Another popular nickname was the Ofenrohr or stove pipe. It was an 8.8.cm reusable anti-tank rocket launcher developed during the latter half of the war.

An Russian ISU-122 tank crosses the Neisse River bound for the Oder in March 1945. Along the Oder and Neisse fronts the Russians began preparing for the final push west to Berlin. General Zhukov's 1st Byelorussian Front and General Konev's 1st Ukrainian Front were preparing to attack German forces defending positions east of Berlin. For the attack the Red Army mustered some 2.5 million men, divided into four armies. They were supported by 41,600 guns and heavy mortars as well as 6,250 tanks and self-propelled guns.

A Wehrmacht soldier inspects damage on a knocked-out Soviet T-34 tank that has been penetrated by a 3.7cm shell.

The second of two photographs showing Wehrmacht troops surveying the same knocked-out Soviet T-34.

Chapter Two

Defence of the Oder

With the Red Army crushing the Vistula front, the only major obstacles between the advancing Soviet forces and Berlin were the River Oder and the Seelow Heights. The defence of the Oder was entrusted to the German 9th Army, which was part of Army Group Vistula.

Plans were drawn up to defend this natural obstacle with everything the Germans could muster. The banks and inland defences were divided into special defensive regions and belts, anti-tank strongpoints, and an extensive network of engineer obstacles. The strength of the German defences varied considerably. Where it was expected that the main attack would take place, German commanders concentrated the largest number of defenders on the narrowest of frontages. In general, each division was able to build five or six defensive belts to a depth of around 4 miles. Although these belts often consisted of little more than lines of trenches with various tank obstacles, other sectors of the front were built into impressive strongholds which included dozens of reinforced machine gun and mortar pits. Each line of defence was mined and protected by barbed wire barriers. Manning these lines were dug-in soldiers armed with an assortment of weapons, ranging from the standard Kar 98k bolt-action rifle to captured Russian guns and Panzerfaust anti-tank rockets. The MG34 and MG42 machine guns were also used extensively. Both were still in ample supply during this late period, but ammunition was a problem. They were installed in pits surrounded by anti-tank obstacles and lines of trenches with various assortments of Pak and artillery guns. The principal anti-tank weapon supplied to the units during this period was the 7.5cm Pak 40, which helped supplement the diminishing numbers of the 8.8cm anti-aircraft gun, but only a handful of them were supplied. The front was stretched, under-armed and under-manned, and soldiers were compelled to defend their positions to the death. The lack of armoured support too was another concern for the German soldier and this brought about considerable apprehension.

During the evening of the 21st, long columns of Russian vehicles, guns and men finally moved forward towards their assembly areas. Thousands of Red Army troops joined other columns until the whole Russian front formed a continuous line of military might. The entire area had become a vast military encampment. Under trees beside roads stood hundreds of anti-aircraft and anti-tank guns, mines and other equipment. Great numbers of armoured vehicles parked in the woods and fields, where trucks, tanks, Katyusha rocket launchers and artillery pieces stood for mile after mile. In total there were some 1,700,000 Red Army soldiers and personnel. Front line strength amounted to some 1,250,000 troops. Most were impatient to end the months of inactivity and begin the battle on which all their thoughts had been focused for so long.

When night fell, units which were to form the first line of attack began drawing up towards the front line. Nearby, the assault detachments moved up and waited anxiously at their jumping-off points. These units consisted of sappers and infantry supported by heavy machine guns, mortars, and a number of tanks and self-propelled guns. Behind the assault detachments came advanced battalions, heavily supported by tank and self-propelled gun battalions.

As the Red Army completed its battle positions, there was a general feeling, not of elation at the thought of mounting the greatest attack thus far on the Eastern Front, but something more deeply ingrained, a desire to expel the invaders from the 'Motherland' forever.

During the early hours of 16 April 1945, the morning was suddenly broken by the shouts of Russian gunnery officers giving orders to begin the artillery barrage along the Oder-Neisse Front. The attack was to soften the German positions and allow easier access for company and battalion sized units.

Shell after shell thundered into the German strongpoints from 22,000 guns and mortars and 2,000 Katyusha multiple rocket launchers. Some German soldiers scrambled in terror out of their trenches to save themselves from the rain of bombs. Destruction also rained down from the air as the Red Army Air Force dived and bombed.

The barrages lasted one or two hours, but in some areas continued longer, and as the infantry moved forward they were supported by a rolling barrage which continued until the troops had captured the first two lines of the German defence.

Many parts of the German front held its position. All morning German defences endured ceaseless fire as the 1st Belorussian Front attacked across the Oder, and the 1st Ukrainian Front attacked across the Neisse. But the first day for the 1st Belorussian Front was a disaster. General Heinrici had anticipated the attack and withdrawn his defenders from the first line of trenches just before the Russian artillery began its barrage.

Over the next twenty-four hours the Germans continued to resist, hindering countless Russian assaults across the boggy terrain and Seelow Heights. By the night of 17 April the German Front was still holding. The following day, both Soviet fronts made steady progress, and by nightfall the 1st Belorussian Front had reached the third and final German line of defence. On the fourth day, 19 April, the 1st Belorussian Front smashed through the last line of the Seelow Heights and began fighting nothing but severely depleted German formations that were slowing withdrawing towards Berlin. The remnants of General Busse's 9th Army, which had been holding the heights, and the remaining northern flank of the 4th Panzer Army, were in danger of being enveloped by elements of the 1st Ukrainian Front.

Some German units remained to defend their positions to the death, but many others, disheartened and frightened, retreated in confusion to avoid the slaughter.

During the initial stages of the attack the Germans found that the Red Army were using new tactics. In other battles the Russians had attacked on a broad front with minimal artillery support. Now they had adopted the German method of concentrating large numbers of infantry supported by heavy artillery and armour. From various observation posts dug along the front the Germans found that the Red Army attacked more heavily defended positions first before bringing up the assault groups. Once the assault groups made contact the armoured forces were then sent in to break through the lines.

The 9th Army, saving themselves from complete annihilation, began withdrawing southwest of Berlin to regroup and defend the capital, while the Russians along the Oder slowly and systematically bulldozed their way forward.

In a trench and these soldiers can be seen armed with the Mauser 7.9mm Kar98k carbine. They are wearing the standard issue splinter design tunics with matching helmet covers.

(**Opposite**) A photograph showing a heavy MG42 machine gun on a sustained fire mount during a defensive action. In battle conditions in open terrain the MG42 team would use their sustained fire mount to protect the flanks of the advancing rifle companies. In built-up areas the crews often had to operate forward with the rifle platoons with light machine gun with bipods only. They were still sometimes able take advantage of the situation and revert back to the heavy machine gun role. Note the Panzerfaust rocket launchers lying at the ready.

(**Above**) Grenadiers armed with the Panzerfaust take cover during a defensive action. By 1945 there was a sharp increase in losses of Russian tanks to the Panzerfaust – more than half the tanks knocked out in combat during the Soviet drive on Berlin were destroyed by Panzerfausts or Panzerschrecks. The high loss became such a concern that the Red Army began installing spaced armour on their tanks. Each tank company was also assigned a platoon of infantry to protect them from infantry anti-tank weapons.

(**Opposite, above**) Along the Oder and an MG42 machine gun unit has set up a defensive position. Across large sectors of the front troops built strongpoints containing light and heavy MG34 and MG42 machine guns positions, anti-tank guns, artillery, and occasionally self-propelled guns. However, many of these defensive positions were often ill-equipped or thinly deployed with not enough ammunition or supplies.

(**Opposite, below**) A Panzerwerfer 42 Maultier rocket launcher crew pose for the camera in front of their vehicle.

(**Above**) An MG34 is positioned on what appears to be a destroyed armoured vehicle. The gunners are probably covering an advancing rifle company. Both soldiers wear the standard army greatcoat.

A troop leader armed with the MP40 moves forward into action. He is wearing the green splinter reversible camouflage winter uniform.

The crew of a 10.5cm field howitzer pause in the action with their weapon. Combat experience showed that artillery support was of decisive importance in both defensive and offensive roles. The three light artillery battalions each had three four-gun batteries with 10.5cm howitzers. A battalion would usually be placed in direct support of an infantry regiment, but did not belong to the regiment.

Wehrmacht troops can be seen advancing through the wreckage of a building. Throughout the defensive fighting on the Eastern front the Germans fought courageously from one receding front to another.

A knocked-out StuG.III in 1945. The StuG.III became a very popular assault gun and was mass produced. The vehicles had initially provided valuable mobile fire support to the infantry, but during 1944 as the Eastern Front receded west, the StuG was primarily used as an anti-tank weapon, thus depriving the infantry of a vital source of fire support. By March/April 1945 most of them were lost in battle or ran out of fuel and were abandoned by their crews.

A typical defensive position in the Oder region. Along the front troops dug slit trenches and set up their weapons in readiness for the advancing enemy. The front would have consisted of MG34 and 42 machine gun emplacements with anti-tank and anti-aircraft positions, and the troops were armed with Panzerfaust and grenades. Often in between these positions were tanks and assault guns. Behind the lines, halftracks and other mobile vehicles carrying troops would support the positions against the advancing enemy.

Wehrmacht troops in their winter splinter insulated garments can be seen laying Teller mines. These mines contained 5.5 kilograms of TNT and were capable of blasting the tracks off any armoured vehicle. They had a fuse activation pressure of about 200 pounds, so only a vehicle or heavy object passing over the mine would set it off.

(**Above**) An MG34 heavy machine gun crew can be seen with their weapon mounted on a sustained fire mount. In open terrain these positions would protect the flanks of advancing rifle companies. However, they were often ill-equipped or too thinly deployed.

(**Opposite, above**) A 15cm Nebelwerfer 41 being prepared and its deadly six-barrelled rocket launchers being fired against an enemy target. This weapon fired 2.5kg shells that could be projected over a range of 7,000 metres. The rockets screamed through the air, causing the enemy to become unnerved by the noise. Initially these weapons served in independent army rocket launcher battalions, and by 1945 they operated as part of regiments and brigades.

(**Opposite, below**) An Sdk.Kfz.251 halftrack in a field. Positioned near it is a GrW.34 8cm mortar crew in action against an enemy target. During the war the mortar had become the standard infantry support weapon giving the soldier valuable high explosive capability beyond the range of riles or grenades.

Two photographs showing a 'Schiessbecher' – 'shooting cup' – grenade launcher being readied for action. This projector was introduced in 1942, designed to be used against infantry, fortifications, and light armoured vehicles. It had a number of special grenades with accompanying propelling cartridges for different tasks. The rifle grenade propelling cartridge fired a wooden projectile that upon impact automatically primed the grenade.

Positioned inside a slit trench are Russian soldiers, one armed with the popular Russian PPSh-41 sub-machine gun, the other with the PTRD-41 Degtyaryov anti-tank rifle. The PPSh sub-machine gun was nicknamed by the Russians as the 'Finka' and was widely used throughout the war, especially during the last months. It was rugged, reliable, and had a large magazine capacity.

Russian soldiers advance across a field towards the German front lines. The Germans were experiencing defensive problems in many areas but still their fortified positions were strong. The Red Army moved forward in their hundreds against them regardless of the cost in life to their own ranks.

Red Army troops hitch a lift onboard a column of T-34 tanks bound for the front lines. By this period of the war the Soviets were vastly superior in their armour against dwindling German army.

(**Opposite, above**) Russian soldiers advance across a field supported by tanks. Despite the best efforts of the German army to bolster its dwindling ranks along the Oder front, nothing could mask the fact that they were dwarfed by the superiority of the Red Army.

(**Above**) A typical strongpoint deployed along the German front comprised mainly of light and heavy MG34 and MG42 machine guns, anti-tank rifle company or battalion, a sapper platoon that was equipped with a host of various explosives, infantry guns, anti-tank artillery company which had a number of anti-tank guns, and occasionally a self-propelled gun.

(**Opposite, below**) Two soldiers in a defensive position on the Oder front. In the distance smoke can be seen rising into the air as fighting intensifies. German forces were determined to hold their positions for as long as possible and prevent the Russians from taking possession of the territory west of the Oder, but they no longer had the manpower, war plant or transportation to effectively do so.

(**Opposite, above**) A company commander in his Wehrmacht green splinter tunic is about to survey the situation through a pair of 6 × 30 Zeiss binoculars.

(**Above**) Between Berlin and the Oder were a mixture of German forces fighting. In this photograph foreign soldiers, which appear to be a machine gun squad, converse. They are wearing the white reversible winter tunic grey side out.

(**Opposite, below**) Panzergrenadiers can be seen on the move across a field. With the mounting losses of men and armour, Panzergrenadiers displayed outstanding ability and endurance in the face of overwhelming odds. Although losses of manpower and equipment had been high, the Germans could still mount small-scale counterattacks.

(**Above**) Panzergrenadiers are seen on the move. Panzergrenadiers were considered elite frontline units and were known for their mobility. Often they would advance into battle with assault guns and other armoured vehicles, which offered them armour protection and mobility until they were close enough to attack enemy positions on foot.

(**Opposite, above**) Inside a ruined building a tank destroyer unit has set up a defensive position in the rubble with their 8.8cm reusable Panzerschreck or rocket tank rifle.

(**Opposite, below**) A 10.5cm heavy field howitzer in a field positioned inside a town. Even as late as 1945 combat experience showed that artillery support was of decisive importance in both defensive and offensive roles.

Chapter Three

Battle of Halbe

With the River Oder breached the Red Army was able to begin a three-front attack towards Berlin sending German forces reeling back towards the Reich capital. What followed was the encirclement of the city. The German 9th Army, which had been fanatically defending the Seelow Heights, was also pushed back by formations of Marshal Ivan Konev's 1st Ukrainian Front on the Neisse. By 20 April, the 9th Army had retreated south-east of Berlin, wrenching open a gap for the 1st Belorussian Front. Konev's forces now threatened 9th Army by two giant pincer movements south and east of Berlin. The southern pincer was composed of the 3rd and 4th Guards Tank Armies, which had already caused considerable disruption penetrating behind the 9th Army front lines in a number of places.

General Busse, commander of 9th Army, was now facing catastrophe, and yet he was not contemplating pulling back. Retreat, except under orders, was tantamount to treason. The Führer, now directing his armies from 50 feet below ground in his bunker below the streets of Berlin, was relying on Busse's army to relieve the city. He appealed to the general saying that 'the 9th Army must hold its position. At the same time, all forces should be made available to try to close the gap with Schörner's units on the southern flank, to set up a continuous front once more.'

By 22 April, Busse's force was almost encircled and close to annihilation. In spite of the Führer's orders, Busse, with the larger half of the 9th Army, consisting of approximately 80,000 soldiers of the XI SS Panzer Corps, the V SS Gebirgsjäger Corps and the garrison of Frankfurt-an-der-Oder, began to withdraw south-westwards towards the Spreewald in an attempt to link up with the Wehrmacht's youngest commander, General Walter Wenck and his 12th Army. Within days the 9th Army, still doggedly battling towards Wenck's forces, was surrounded and being continuously hammered night and day by Russian ground and aerial forces. The supply situation was dire. The Luftwaffe attempted a number of airdrops, but they were limited and unsuccessful. As a result, the entire northern flank of the 9th Army collapsed. The remnants of the army then retreated along roads, tracks and fields to escape the slaughter. Vehicles were abandoned along the way as they ran out of fuel. During their escape, the exhausted troops moved into a forest near the large village of Halbe. It was here that remnants of the 9th Army would endure what survivors called 'the slaughter at Halbe'.

The Halbe Forest was half an hour's drive south-east of Berlin and consisted of 17 acres of pine trees and forest land. Here approximately 80,000 troops from Busse's Army had withdrawn in a desperate attempt to link up with Wenck's 12th Army. As the 9th Army withdrew, troops of the 1st Belorussian Front and the 1st Ukrainian Front followed in their wake leaving a trail of devastation. What followed was total horror as the Russians closed in around the forest. Sixteen-rail Katyusha rocket launchers were positioned around the perimeter and for hours a storm of fire was poured onto the Germans trapped inside. Busse could not hold the Russians back, nor could he counter-attack properly because he had dispersed what little artillery and armour he had available to give each fighting unit a chance to break out west and surrender to the Allies instead of to the Russians. Ignoring Hitler's orders to 'stand fast' on morning of 26th April, leading elements of the 9th Army advanced through Halbe and found two Russian armies. They crossed the autobahn and reached the Baruth–Zossen road, which was a vital supply line to Russian forces in south-western districts of Berlin. Soon the German troops crashed into lines of enemy resistance and heavy fighting ensued. Soviet forces were strong and as a result forced German formations back across the autobahn and into the Halbe Forest.

During the night and the next day, 27 April, units of 9th Army renewed their attacks. In the south from Halbe through towards Baruth, and in the north from Teupitz, thousands of soldiers supported by a handful of tanks assaulted Russian positions. The fighting was again vicious and both sides suffered heavy casualties. Throughout the 27th, Russian aircraft and artillery fire intensified. The Germans again attempted to break out on 28 April. Busse's men were spread out, with groups around Halbe, and others stretching all the way back to Storkow, where rearguard fighting was raging against Zhukov's men. During the fighting westwards, the Germans smashed through the line held by the 50th Guards Rifle Division. Angered by the breakout attempt, Genera Konev was determined to destroy the 9th Army once and for all. Air divisions supporting the 1st Ukrainian Front flew some 2,500 attack missions and 1,700 bombing sorties to attempt to blunt the breakout. Russian forces attacked the village of Halbe from the south with artillery and Katyushas. But the Germans fought on.

By the next day, 29 April, German units had virtually no artillery or ammunition left. There were few machine guns and almost no bullets, but still units made suicidal efforts to break out of the forest to link up with Wenck. Those who succeeded trudged westwards under constant Russian fire. Exhausted and depleted of arms some 25,000 German soldiers managed to claw their way out and escape to join up with the 12th Army on the eastern side of Reichstrasse 2, the road running north-south through Beelitz.

The 9th Army was supposed to have relieved Berlin, but instead had been surrounded and virtually annihilated. Amazingly, a quarter of the army that had moved into the Halbe area had linked up with Wenck. The rest were either captured, killed or surrounded.

Remnants of the 9th Army were again surrounded west of Luckenwalde by the north-westerly thrust of the Russian 4th Guards Tank Army, a few miles from 12th Army troops. The remainder of the combined German 9th and 12th Armies then retreated westwards towards the Elbe River, leaving Berlin to fight out its last days on its own.

Wehrmacht troops advance across a field hauling three captured Russian Maxim machine guns.

Two photographs showing a well camouflaged StuG.III on a forest road with its crew. By this period of the war the StuG had been absorbed into Panzer units, Panzer and Panzergrenadier divisions of the Wehrmacht and Waffen-SS, having performed sterling service in action.

German troops are taking evasive cover from Russian bombing. Strewn around their trench are stick grenades in preparation for an enemy infantry attack. They are all wearing green splinter reversible tunics. Note the platoon leader armed with the MP40 machine pistol with a stick grenade stuck into his black leather infantryman's belt.

A PaK gunner is surveying the terrain ahead using a pair of 6 × 30 Zeiss binoculars. He is positioned next to the muzzle brake of a 7.5cm PaK40. The PaK40's effectiveness on the battlefield made it a very popular weapon with the German troops, but there were never enough of them. The PaK40 was a powerful and deadly weapon, especially in the hands of well-trained operators.

Firing from a pit is a mortar crew equipped with the 8cm sGrW 34 mortar. Defensive positions now consisted of a motley collection of mortars, tanks, PaK and flaK guns. Behind these positions at varying depths were anti-tank defences, including more mortars, Panzerschreck, Panzerfaust, a handful of 7.5cm and 8.8cm PaK guns, ready to counter any enemy units that managed to break through.

From a typical dugout a soldier can be seen making his way along a trench during intensive fighting. Much of the German front consisted of miles of trenches and various other types of position, to defend against poundings from Russian artillery that could last for days on end.

Two young soldiers, wearing winter reversibles grey side out, are taking cover from fighting. Out on the front lines many of the troops were already fatigued, low on ammunition and equipment and would soon be unable to defend their positions with much success.

A platoon leader converses with one of his men during the Halbe operation in March 1945. The men are all wearing the standard issue army greatcoat and appear to be taking refuge in a bunker.

(**Opposite, above**) Taking cover in undergrowth, a soldier is armed with the Panzerschreck, Raketenpanzerbuchse, or rocket tank rifle, RPzB.

(**Opposite, below**) A number of Waffen-SS soldiers are seen on the march through undergrowth watched by other troops resting. Note that the soldiers are carrying Kar 98K carbines from fallen patrol members. Also of interest that the leading soldier is carrying the Soviet 14.5mm PTRD-41 anti-tank rifle.

(**Above**) A photograph taken the moment a German 8cm sGrW mortar crew go into action against an enemy target. In order to keep the mortar steady during firing two of the ammunition handlers would hold the tripod. This mortar earned a deadly reputation on the Eastern Front and was used extensively during the last battles before Berlin.

(**Above, left**) A young grenadier armed with the Panzerfaust. The Panzerfaust literally meant armour fist. The weapon was an inexpensive, recoilless anti-tank weapon that was mass produced during the second half of the war. It consisted of a small, disposable preloaded launch tube which fired a high explosive shaped charge, and could be operated by one single soldier. Various models of the Panzerfaust remained in service throughout the latter part of the war.

(**Above, right**) Watched by his comrades a soldier is taught how to use the Panzerfaust. More than half of the Russian tanks knocked out in combat were destroyed by Panzerfausts or Panzerschrecks.

(**Opposite, below**) An 8cm sGrW mortar crew during a pause in the fighting. In 1944 there was a platoon of four 8cm mortars assigned to a grenadier battalion's machine gun company. However, by March 1945 this had halved or become virtually non-existent. But the Germans found the mortar so effective that they often used captured Soviet mortars and fired their own ammunition from them using German firing tables.

(**Opposite, below**) A photograph of a grenadier armed with the famous StG 44 Sturmgewehr 44 assault rifle 44, or StG 44 for short. These assault rifles were used primarily to counter the Soviet PPS and PPSh-41 sub-machine gun, which used the 7.62 × 25mm Tokarev round.

Three photographs showing the crew of a 7.5cm PaK 40 anti-tank gun preparing to engage a Soviet tank. These weapons were normally assigned to divisional anti-tank battalions, but by 1945 they were usually assigned to grenadier regiment anti-tank battalions.

Well kitted Panzergrenadiers are seen foraging in the woodland looking for items to build a shelter. At least two of them are armed with the MP40 machine pistol, normally issued to squad or platoon leaders. Each of their ammunition pouches holds three 32-round magazines.

(**Opposite, above**) A soviet artillery crew are moving their 76mm M1936 artillery gun to the forward edge of a field to begin a fire mission against German positions.

(**Opposite, below**) A well concealed MG42 machine gunner in some undergrowth. The MG42 proved its capabilities in both offensive and defensive actions. Its dependability was second to none and every unit of the German army and Waffen-SS was equipped with it. By 1945 many units had become totally dependent on them to hold back the attacking enemy.

(**Above**) An action scene showing Russian troops rushing into action. This photograph, as with much of the wartime imagery photographed by the Red Army, was staged for propaganda purposes. Note the soldier armed with the much valued and effective Soviet 14.5mm PTRD-41 anti-tank rifle.

(**Above**) Once again, another staged Soviet photograph showing a Russian 50mm light infantry mortar. Interestingly, the barrel was clamped at two elevation angles only: 45 and 75 degrees. Range variations were made by altering a sleeve round the base of the barrel as seen in this photograph. This sleeve opened a series of gas ports which bled off exhaust gases which determined the range.

(**Opposite, above**) Dejected German PoWs from Busse's 9th Army are seen being moved to a detainment area to a fate that can only be imagined. It was the 9th Army that was supposed to have relieved Berlin, but instead under unrelenting Russian firepower, it was pushed back, surrounded and virtually annihilated. A quarter of the army that had moved into the Halbe area managed to link up with General Wenck, but the rest were either captured, killed or surrounded. This is part of its remnants.

(**Opposite, below**) A photograph showing Russian soldiers with a captured German commanding officer during operations outside Berlin in early April 1945. Behind them is a column of Russian infantry moving towards the front.

A dejected column of refugees, both on foot and on horse-drawn transport, are seen moving along a very congested road. Intermingled are PoWs. Note the line of Russian armour parked beside the road.

Chapter Four

Battle for Berlin

By 20 April, Hitler's birthday, the military situation in front of Berlin was calamitous, and it was fast becoming clear, even to the least informed German soldier, how rapidly their army was diminishing. Absence of communications made it impossible for the Germans to accurately access the extent of their disintegration, but they were stunned by the weight of the blow that had hit Army Group Vistula, and then the Oder and Neisse fronts. Areas that still remained in German hands were slowly reduced to a few shrinking pockets of resistance. Despite many appeals for reinforcements, no troops arrived. Berlin, was now on its own.

On 20 April 1945, the Red Army war machine celebrated Hitler's 56th birthday with a an artillery barrage by the 1st Belorussian Front, so massive that it was greater than the tonnage dropped by Western Allied bombers on the city. General Konev then ordered his two powerful tank armies, the 3rd and 4th Guards, to break into Berlin. Fighting was bitter and relentless.

As the Russians slowly battered their way through the suburbs, on 23 April Hitler appointed General Helmuth Weidling commander of the Berlin defence area. On this day, Chuikov's rifle units begun crossing the Spree and Dahme Rivers south of Kopenick. The following day bitter fighting raged as Weidling's LVI Panzer Corps became embroiled in fighting with the Soviet 5th Shock Army.

By 25 April Berlin was surrounded, and the next day approximately 500,000 Soviet troops bulldozed their way through the city. Weidling tried his best to stop the Russian advance with his force of 45,000 soldiers who were under-armed and weakened, and 5,000 Luftwaffe personnel and Hitlerjugend, all armed with hand-held weapons.

In the centre of the city in the government district, SS Brigadeführer Wilhelm Mohnke had the unenviable task of defending the Reich Chancellery and the Führerbunker. He had 2,000 men under his command. The city's defence was broken into eight sectors, designated 'A' to 'H', each one having a separate command. To the north was the 9th Fallschirmjäger Division, to the north-east was Panzer Division Müncheberg, in the west was the 20th Infantry Division, south-east and to the east of Tempelhof Airport was the 11th SS Panzergrenadier Division Nordland. All the reserves were deployed in Berlin's central district, comprising mainly of the

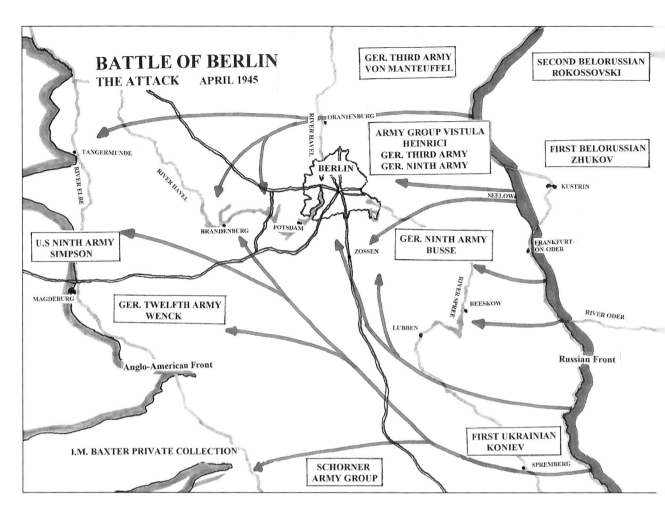

BATTLE OF BERLIN
THE ATTACK   APRIL 1945

GER. THIRD ARMY
VON MANTEUFFEL

SECOND BELORUSSIAN
ROKOSSOVSKI

ORANIENBURG

RIVER HAVEL

TANGERMUNDE

ARMY GROUP VISTULA
HEINRICI
GER. THIRD ARMY
GER. NINTH ARMY

FIRST BELORUSSIAN
ZHUKOV

RIVER ELBE

RIVER HAVEL

BERLIN

KUSTRIN

SEELOW

BRANDENBURG   POTSDAM

GER. NINTH ARMY
BUSSE

FRANKFURT-
ON-ODER

U.S NINTH ARMY
SIMPSON

ZOSSEN

RIVER SPREE

MAGDEBURG

GER. TWELFTH ARMY
WENCK

BEESKOW

RIVER ODER

LUBBEN

Russian Front

Anglo-American Front

I.M. BAXTER PRIVATE COLLECTION

FIRST UKRAINIAN
KONIEV

SPREMBERG

SCHORNER
ARMY GROUP

18th Panzergrenadier Division and later by a small contingent of French SS volunteers under the command of SS Brigadeführer Gustav Krukenberg.

For the next week the battle for Berlin raged. German troops were ordered to fight to the death and anyone found deserting or shirking their duties was hunted down by Himmler's personal escort battalion and hanged from the nearest lamppost.

Supplies were desperately low. There were no less than fifteen different types of rifle and ten kinds of machine gun, many of which had been salvaged from a number of occupied countries, but the average ammunition supply was about five rounds per rifle. Fighters aged 10 and over 60 were expected to defend their positions with these guns against enemy troops which were often supported by the mighty T-34 tank. Those fortunate enough to be armed with the Panzerfaust stood more of a chance. Where resistance was particularly determined, the whole area was saturated with Katyusha rocket fire, and then the tanks would go in to take out the dazed survivors with machine gun fire and high explosive. Many of the captured and wounded were executed on the spot and left suspended from the lampposts as a warning to others if they resisted.

All over the city bloody battles continued in the smoke and brick dust. Even when they found themselves cut off on an island of rubble, Germans still stubbornly refused to surrender. As a result, Red Army troops would spend whole days clearing a street. The Germans had become masters in the technique of house-to-house combat. In the burning ruins of the city they had developed 'killing zones', where small units were ordered to defend every square yard with machine guns, mortars, grenades, flame throwers, explosive charges, or whatever they had. Some street fighting assault squads were armed with spades and knives for silent killing, while other more special-ised soldiers were assigned to sniper units. In the parklands too, tank crews camou-flaged their Panzers and soldiers disguised their anti-tank guns, burying them in rubble or mounds of earth. All approaches were mined and up to thirty sappers would lie in wait in a position. Experienced ones would run out of cover and drop a mine in front of an advancing tank.

On 26 April Soviet forces smashed their way through the southern suburbs of the city and attacked the Tempelhof Airport. The Red Army then continued its push and met spirited resistance from the Müncheberg Division. However, by the next day both the Müncheberg and Nordland divisions, defending the south-east of Berlin, were confronted by four massive Soviet armies – the 8th Guards Army, the 1st and 3rd Guards Tank Armies, and the 5th Shock Army. The German divisions were pushed back into the centre of the burning city and took up positions around Hermannplatz.

The fighting was intense, sometimes hand-to-hand, and in the early hours of 29 April reports reached Hitler's bunker that Moltke bridge had been captured and crossed by the 3rd Shock Army. Red Army troops were seen crossing the streets and assaulting various buildings including the Ministry of the Interior. Later that morning the Russians captured the Gestapo headquarters on Prinz-Albrecht Strasse. To the south-west the 8th Guards fought in a series of heavy clashes along Landwehr canal into the Tiergarten.

The next day, 30 April, the Russians began their attack on the Reichstag. All day Red Army soldiers fought against well defended German soldiers that were sup-ported by flak guns. It was not until the evening that the Russians entered the building and began fighting room to room. The defence of the capital had shrunk to a small area in the city centre defended by about 10,000 exhausted and mauled German soldiers, who were now being assaulted from all sides and slowly battered into submission.

The following day, 1 May, news reached some German command posts, though most soldiers never received these reports, that the 'Führer had died while leading his troops in the final defence of Berlin.' In fact Hitler had killed himself the day before in his bunker. News of his death sent shock waves across the command chain, and in some sectors brought about immediate surrender. By the next day, 2 May, Berlin had fallen, apart from a few fanatical hold-outs in some parts of the city.

According to Russian reports it was estimated that 81,000 Red Army soldiers were killed during the battle for Berlin, including in the Oder-Seelow Heights and Halbe operations. A further 280,000 were reported wounded or sick during this time. As for the Germans, the Russians claimed that 480,000 troops were killed and captured, but the German claimed this number to be 100,000. The loss in civilians is unknown, but casualties were estimated at 125,000.

(**Above**) Russian artillery begin their preliminary bombardment of the suburbs of Berlin in April 1945.

(**Opposite**) A soldier hands some rations to a grenadier during urban fighting. The soldiers are wearing standard Zeltbahn waterproof capes and their steel helmets are covered with foliage.

An interesting photograph showing a soldier being presented the Knight's Cross of the Iron Cross by his divisional commander. The award of the Knight's Cross to enlisted men was quite a rare occurrence, and got rarer towards the end of the war.

A young soldier who has just received the Knight's Cross is congratulated by one of his men, an NCO. Of interest, note on the soldier's left breast is a wound badge (silver for three or four wounds, or for a serious single wound), Iron Cross 1st Class, Armour Battle Badge, and above the pocket is the Close Battle Clasp.

Two photographs showing knocked-out Jagdpanzer IVs – 'Guderian Ducks'.

(**Above**) Volkssturm recruits with the Panzerfaust slung over their shoulders. Virtually all the Volkssturm conscripts that entered service during the latter part of the war were not properly trained and lacked battlefield experience. Although many were filled with courage and determination, they were no match against well-seasoned Soviet troops that had marched and battled their way across hundreds of miles to the gates of Berlin.

(**Opposite, above**) A column of Russian tanks with troops hitching a lift advance through the rubble-strewn suburbs of Berlin in April 1945.

(**Opposite, below**) Negotiating a Berlin street, which can clearly be seen for barricades of buses strewn across the road, is a halftrack and a motorcycle. The halftrack undoubtedly transformed the fighting quality of the infantry during the war and enabled them to better support the advancing armoured spearheads. In close quarter urban fighting however, armoured vehicles such as the halftrack were less manoeuvrable and were easy targets for the enemy.

(**Opposite, above**) A knocked-out Pz.Kpfw.IV sits in the rubble of a decimated street. The vehicle's side skirts have completely been lost. The skirts were constructed of mild steel plates and were very effective against close-range anti-tank rifles and high explosive shells.

(**Opposite, below**) A photograph showing two troops in a defensive position during operations in Berlin. Note the Panzerschreck laying on a mound of earth ready for action at a moment's notice. Defensive positions erected like this were very common across the city.

(**Above**) A grenadier is seen dismounting from the side of a damaged building. For the German army defending Berlin, the military situation was calamitous, and it was clear by early April 1945 how rapidly their army was diminishing. The absence of communications too made it impossible for the Germans to access the full extent of their disintegration. There seemed no stopping the tide of the Russian advance, and as they remorselessly pushed forward into the suburbs of the city, German soldiers became increasingly confused and entangled in bitter bloody fighting.

Five photographs showing the extent of damage in the suburbs of Berlin including one of the rail lines. In spite of overwhelming superiority of the enemy the Germans still fought fiercely and determinedly in the ruins of the city, while Berliners still continued to live and hope they would survive the battle.

(**Below**) German PoWs shuffle across a bridge over the River Oder and are taken to the rear of the 1st Ukrainian Front. It was the 1st Ukrainian Front that had provided the defence against the counter-attacks by Army Wenck, which had been tasked to relieve Berlin and the 9th Army.

Wehrmacht soldiers armed with a Karbiner 98K bolt action rifle, the standard German infantry weapon used throughout the war, are seen rushing from one building to another during operations inside the city.

(**Above**) A Russian T34 tank negotiates a street with some soldiers onboard. German defenders of the city were determined at all costs to knock out as many Red Army tanks as possible, but the constant onslaught of the massive tank armadas meant that in spite of heavy Russian losses there were always more tanks to replace them.

(**Opposite, above**) Two Red Army troops rush along a Berlin street passing a burning building during the battle for Berlin. The machine gunner on the left is hauling his Russian Maxim 10 machine gun, while the other infantryman is armed with the famous PPAh-1941 sub-machine gun.

(**Opposite, below**) A Red Army tank during an operation along a Berlin street. Fighting in the city was intense and in spite of the high tank losses, ever more Soviet tanks were brought in. Often tanks blasted buildings that were being defended by Germans troops. This frequently reduced the time and losses to Russian soldiers undertaking long-drawn-out house-to-house battles.

A German soldier is seen here in a defensive position inside the city. A discarded German teller mine can be seen lying next to his slit trench among other spares and battlefield booty.

(**Opposite, above**) A column of Red Army troops advance along a bombed-out street. In only a matter of days of the Russians advancing through the suburbs of Berlin they had turned many acres of the city into burned and devastated wastelands of death.

(**Opposite, below**) Russian artillery during a pause in the battle in the centre of Berlin in late April 1945. Russian soldiers had adopted a simple method of switching their attention from one area of the city to another, battering from one block to another by blasting the streets into rubble using artillery and tanks.

(**Opposite, above**) A 'still' from a Russian film showing Soviet troops embroiled in a street battle in the heart of Berlin. Losses for the Germans at this stage of the battle were huge and its forces inside and outside the capital were facing a major catastrophe, and yet, retreat, except under orders, was tantamout to treason. Hitler's orders were to stand fast come what may.

(**Opposite, below**) Nicknamed by the Germans 'Stalin's sledgehammer', this powerful and deadly 203mm howitzer M1931 (B-4) was primarily used against fortifications and in street fighting for destroying buildings and bunkers. A number of these howitzers were used during the battle for Berlin.

(**Above**) Berliners are seen along a street. Note the complete destruction in the area. By late April there were almost no supplies of food and no water or electricity. A number of districts were so heavily bombed that with no amenities of food Berliners were actually beginning to starve.

(**Opposite, above**) Two Soviet soldiers are seen with their field telephones on a Berlin street. Behind them painted across a wall is 'Berlin bleibt Deutsch' – Berlin remains German.

(**Above**) Russian artillery gunners preparing their M1942 ZIS-76mm gun for action along a Berlin street. Often artillery or anti-tank weapons were deployed on street corners or along main roads.

(**Opposite, below**) A photograph purposely staged showing Russian soldiers, one joyously playing his accordion in front of a wall, with German graffiti painted in white, 'Berlin remains German'. This slogan was coined by Goebbels.

(**Above**) A photograph showing the death and destruction of the battle for Berlin. Dead soldiers can be seen scattered in the ruins along a main road into the city centre. Inside the city, despite overwhelming enemy superiority, the Germans fought a fanatical resistance and remained formidable opponents, fighting for every bridge, street, road, and building. But to the German soldier the defence of the Reich capital was no normal defence. They knew very well that the Russians were determined to exact vengeance on them.

(**Opposite, above**) In the city centre and a Russian artillery gunner raises his arm in preparation for another fire mission against the German defenders. Spread out across the square various artillery pieces can be seen including the Russian 152mm M1937 howitzer.

(**Opposite, below**) Russian T-34 tanks hurtle along a street watched by curious but nervous Berliners at the side of the road. The commanders are clearly visible out of their turret hatches, suggesting that the fighting is over in this area.

(**Opposite, above**) Soviet troops inside a typical German home during street fighting. Faced with the prospect of Russian occupation, many German families fled their homes with their valuables, and some even chose suicide rather than live under Soviet rule.

(**Above**) A staged Russian photograph showing Soviet troops during an infantry attack during the battle for Berlin, although this image was more than likely taken after the fall of the capital.

(**Opposite, below**) Berliners are seen walking along a thoroughfare inside the city passing a stationary Soviet truck mounting an M13 16-rail rocket launcher. The rockets that were used were not a precision weapon but were used to saturate an area with explosion and fire. They were much feared by the Germans, as the rockets had a terrifying screaming whistle.

(**Above**) A Berliner has come out of hiding and sits among the ruins of his city. Abandoned behind him is a Russian artillery tractor. This was used to move heavy armour from one part of the line to another.

(**Opposite, above**) Grenadiers and a Fallschirmjäger soldier (far left) stand together in a street. Their reversible suits are very dirty. Note their rifles, all with fixed optical sights. Optical sights were often used during urban or close-quarter operations where soldiers sometimes had to remain in fixed positions for long periods of time.

(**Opposite, below**) A Soviet soldier waves a flag on top of a Russian ISU-152 tank to communicate with forward Russian units not to open fire, indicating that they have secured the area. Passing the stationary tank are German PoWs.

(**Opposite, above**) A column of Soviet IS2 tanks are seen in front of the Brandenburg Gate at the end of April 1945. The IS2's powerful 122mm M1943 gun could penetrate the thick, angled frontal armour of the German Panther tank, which was arguably the best all round tank of the war. During the battle for Berlin these tanks were very successful, their thick armour plating making them invulnerable to all but the largest calibre anti-tank guns.

(**Opposite, below**) An interesting photograph showing a T-34 85 operating in front of the Brandenburg Gate at the end of April 1945. Note the cages attached to the vehicle to prevent enemy troops from climbing onboard or attaching anti-tank mines.

(**Above**) An abandoned Tiger tank is seen near the Brandenburg Gate at the end of the battle for Berlin. The Tiger was a very successful heavy tank, but in urban and close-quarter fighting it was not versatile. Those that operated inside the city, and there were only a handful, were soon lost, or ran out of fuel or ammunition and were abandoned.

Two photographs showing captured German troops. During the battle for Berlin German forces consisted of Hitlerjugend, Volkssturm, Luftwaffe personnel, Fallschirmjäger, Wehrmacht and Waffen-SS soldiers.

Captured Hitlerjugend soldiers smile for the camera following their capture in April 1945. (*NARA*)

Two photographs taken in sequence showing a knocked-out StuG assault gun in the ruins of a post-war Berlin.

A post-war photograph showing the bombed and blasted old government building, the Reichstag. Following the surrender of the city, it would be 44 years later that Berlin would once more become the German capital.

Appendix

Order of Battle

German Order of Battle for the Defence of Berlin

OKW RESERVE (later allocated to the LVI Panzer Corps, 9th Army)

18th Panzergrenadier Division (General Josef Rauch)

30th & 51st Panzergrenadier Regts

118th Panzer Regt (part)

18th Artillery Regt

ARMY GROUP 'VISTULA' (General Gotthard Heinrici)

III SS 'Germanic' Panzer Corps (SS General Felix Steiner)

9th Army

11th SS 'Nordland' Panzergrenadier Division (SS General Jurgen Ziegler/SS General Gustav Krukenberg)

23rd 'Norge' Panzergrenadier Regt

24th 'Danmark' Panzergrenadier Regt

11th SS 'Hermann von Salza' Panzer Battalion

11th SS 'Nordland' Armoured Reconnaissance Battalion

503rd SS Heavy Tank Battalion

23rd SS 'Nederland' Panzergrenadier Division (SS General Wagner)

3rd Panzer Army (General Hasso von Manteuffel)

'Swinemünde' Corps

402nd & 2nd Naval Divisions

XXXII Corps

'Voigt' & 281st Infantry Divisions

549th Volksgrenadier Division

Stettin Garrison

'Oder' Corps

610th & 'Klossek' Infantry Divisions

XXXXVI Panzer Corps

547th Volksgrenadier Division

1st Naval Division (Later Divisions to join 3rd Panzer Army)

27th SS 'Langemarck' Grenadier Division

28th SS 'Wallonien' Grenadier Division

9th Army (General Theodor Busse)

156th Infantry Division

541st Volksgrenadier Division

404th Volks Artillery Corps

406th Volks Artillery Corps

408th Volks Artillery Corps

CI Corps

5th Light Infantry Division

606th Infantry Division

309th 'Berlin' Infantry Division

25th Panzergrenadier Division

111th SPG Training Brigade

'1001 Nights' Combat Group

LVI Panzer Corps (General Helmuth Weidling)

9th Fallschirmjäger Division
25th, 26th & 27th Fallschirmjäger Regiment
9th Fallschirmjäger Artillery Regiment
20th Panzergrenadier Division
76th & 90th Panzergrenadier Regiment
8th Panzer Battalion
20th Artillery Regiment

'Müncheberg' Panzer Division
1st & 2nd 'Müncheberg' Panzergrenadier
  Regiment
'Müncheberg' Panzer Regiment
'Müncheberg' Armoured Artillery Regiment
920th SPG Training Brigade

XI SS Panzer Corps (SS General Mathias Kleinheisterkamp)

303rd 'Döberitz' Infantry Division
169th Infantry Division
712th Infantry Division

'Kurmark' Panzergrenadier Division
502nd SS Heavy Tank Battalion

Frankfurt an der Oder Garrison (General Ernst Biehler)

V SS Mountain Corps

SS General Friedrich Jackeln
286th Infantry Division
32nd SS '30 Januar' Volksgrenadier Division

391st Sy Division
561st SS Tank Hunting Battalion

ARMY GROUP CENTRE (Field Marshal Ferdinand Schörner)

4th Panzer Army (General Fritz-Herbert Gräser)
(later transferred to the 9th Army)

V Corps (General Wagner)

35th SS Police Grenadier Division
36th SS Grenadier Division
275th Infantry Division

342nd Infantry Division
21st Panzer Division

12th Army (General Walter Wenck)

XX Corps (General Carl-Erik Koehler)

'Theodor Körner' RAD Division
'Ulrich von Hutten' Infantry Division

'Ferdinand von Schill' Infantry Division
'Scharnhorst' Infantry Division

XXXIX Panzer Corps (General Karl Arndt)

12–21 April 1945 under OKW with the
following structure:
  'Clausewitz' Panzer Division 'Schlageter'
    RAD Division
  84th Infantry Division

21–26 April 1945 under 12th Army with the
following structure:
  'Clausewitz' Panzer Division
  84th Infantry Division
  'Hamburg' Reserve Infantry Division
  'Meyer' Infantry Division

XXXXI Panzer Corps (General Rudolf Holste)

'Von Hake' Infantry Division

199th Infantry Division

'V-Weapons' Infantry Division

1st HJ Tank Destroyer Brigade

'Hermann Göring' Jagdpanzer Brigade

XXXXVIII Panzer Corps (General Maximilian von Edelsheim)

14th Flak Division

'Leipzig' Battle Group

'Halle' Battle Group

Ad-hoc Formations

'Friedrich Ludwig Jahn' RAD Division
(Col Gerhard Klein/Col Franz Weller)

'Potsdam' Infantry Division (Col Erich Lorenz)

Soviet Order of Battle Attack on Berlin

2nd Byelorussian Front (Marshal K.K. Rokossovsky)

2nd Shock Army (General I.I. Fedyurinsky)
108th & 116th Rifle Corps

65th Army (General P.I. Batov)
18th, 46th & 105th Rifle Corps

70th Army (General V.S. Popov)
47th, 96th & 114th Rifle Corps

49th Army (General I.T. Grishin)
70th & 121st Rifle Corps
191st, 200th & 330th Rifle Divisions

19th Army
40th Guards, 132nd & 134th Rifle Corps

5th Guards Tank Army

29th Tank Corps

1st Tank & 4th Mechanised Brigades

4th Air Army
4th Air Assault, 5th Air Bomber and 8th Air Fighter Corps

1st Byelorussian Front (Marshal G.K. Zhukov)

61st Army
9th Guards, 80th & 89th Rifle Corps

1st Polish Army

1st, 2nd, 3rd, 4th & 6th Polish Infantry
   Divisions
1st Polish Cavalry Brigade

4th Polish Heavy Tank Brigade
13th Polish SP Assault Artillery Brigade
7th Polish Assault Artillery Battalion

47th Army
77th, 125th & 129th Rifle Corps
70th Guards Independent Tank Regt

3rd Shock Army
7th Rifle Corps
146th, 265th & 364th Rifle Divisions
12th Guards Rifle Corps

79th Rifle Corps
150th Rifle Division
469th, 674th & 756th Rifle Regiments
171st Rifle Division

9th Tank Corps
23rd, 95th & 108th Tank Brigades
8th Motorised Rifle Regt

5th Shock Army

9th Rifle Corps
230th, 248th & 301st Rife Divisions

26th Guards Corps
89th Guards, 94th Guards & 266th Rifle Divisions

32nd Rifle Corps
60th Guards, 295th & 416th Rifle Divisions
11th, 67th Guards & 220th Tank Brigades

8th Guards Army

4th Guards Rifle Corps
35th Guards, 47th Guards & 57th Guards Rifle Divisions

28th Guards Rifle Corps
39th Guards, 79th Guards & 88th Guards Rifle Divisions

29th Guards Rifle Corps
27th Guards, 74th Guards & 82nd Guards
   Rifle Divisions
7th Guards Tank Brigade
84th Guards, 65th & 259th Independent Tank
   Regiments

334th, 1204th, 1416th, 1825th & 1892nd SP
   Assault Artillery Regiments

23rd Guards, 52nd Guards & 33rd Rifle
   Divisions

380th, 525th & 783rd Rifle Regiments
207th Rifle Division
594th, 597th & 598th Rifle Regiments

1455th & 1508th SP Assault Artillery
   Regiments

92nd Independent Tank Regiment
396th Guards & 1504th SP Assault Artillery
   Regiments

371st, 374th Guards, 694th, 1026th, 1061st,
   1087th & 1200th SP Assault Artillery
   Regiments

69th Army
25th, 61st & 91st Rifle Corps
117th & 283rd Rifle Divisions
68th Tank Brigade

12th SP Assault Artillery Brigade
344th Guards, 1205th, 1206th &
1221st SP Assault Artillery Regiments

33rd Army
16th, 38th & 62nd Rifle Corps
2nd Guards Cavalry Corps
95th Rifle Division

257th Independent Tank Regiment
360th & 361st SP Assault Artillery Regiments

16th Air Army
6th & 9th Air Assault Corps
3rd & 6th Air Bomber Corps
1st Guards, 3rd, 6th & 13th Air Fighter Corps
1st Guards, 240th, 282nd & 286th Air Fighter
   Divisions
2nd & 11th Guards Air Assault Divisions
113th, 183rd, 188th & 221st Air Bomber
   Divisions

9th Guards & 242nd Air Night Bomber
   Divisions
16th & 72nd Air Reconnaissance Regiments
93rd & 98th Air Observation Regiments
176th Guards Air Fighter Regiments
226th Air Transport Regiments

18th Air Army
1st Guards, 2nd, 3rd & 4th Air Bomber Corps
45th Air Bomber Division

56th Air Fighter Division
742nd Air Reconnaissance Regt

1st Guards Tank Army

8th Guards Mechanised Corps
19th, 20th & 21st Guards Mechanised Brigades
1st Guards Tank Brigades
48th Guards Tank Regiments

353rd & 400th Guards SP Assault Artillery
   Regiments
8th Guards M/C Battalion

11th Guards Tank Corps
40th, 44th & 45th Guards Tank Brigades
27th Guards Mechanised Brigade

362nd, 399th Guards & 1454 SP Assault
   Artillery Regiments
9th Guards M/C Battalion

11th Tank Corps
20th, 36th & 65th Tank Brigades
12th Motorised Rifle Brigade
50th Guards Tank Regiment
1461st & 1493rd SP Assault Artillery
   Regiments

64th Guards Tank Brigade
19th SP Assault Artillery Brigade
11th Guards Independent Tank Regiment
12th Guards M/C Battalion

2nd Guards Tank Army

1st Mechanised Corps
19th, 35th & 37th Mechanised Brigades
219th Tank Brigades

347th Guards, 75th & 1822nd SP Assault
   Artillery Regiments
57th M/C Battalion

9th Guards Tank Corps
47th, 50th & 65th Guards Tank Brigades
33rd Guards Mechanised Brigade

341st, 369th & 386th Guards SP Assault
   artillery Regiments
17th Guards M/C Battalion

12th Guards Tank Corps
48th, 49th & 66th Guards Tank Brigades
34th Guards Mechanised Brigades
79th Guards Tank Regiments
387th & 393rd Guards SP Assault Artillery
   Regiments

6th Guards Independent Tank Regiments
5th Guards M/C Regiment
16th Guards M/C Battalion

3rd Army
35th, 40th & 41st Rifle Corps
1812th, 1888th & 1901st SP Assault Artillery
   Regiments
2nd, 3rd & 7th Guards Cavalry Corps

3rd & 8th Guards Tank Corps
244th Independent Tank Regiment
31st, 39th, 51st & 55th Independent
   Armoured Train Battalion

3rd Guards Army
21st, 76th & 120th Rifle Corps
25th Tank Corps
389th Rifle Division

87th Guards Independent Tank Regiment
938th SP Assault Artillery Regiment

13th Army
24th, 27th & 102nd Rifle Corps
88th Independent Tank Regiment

327th, 372nd Guards, 768th & 1228th SP
   Assault Artillery Regiment

5th Guards Army
32nd, 33rd & 34th Guards Rifle Corps

4th Guards Tank Corps

2nd Polish Army
5th, 7th, 8th, 9th & 10th Polish Infantry
   Divisions
1st Polish Tank Corps

16th Polish Tank Brigade
5th Polish Independent Tank Regiment
28th polish SP Assault Artillery Regiment

52nd Army
48th, 73rd & 78th Rifle Corps
7th Guards Mechanised Corps
213th Rifle Division

8th SP Assault Artillery Brigade
124th Independent Tank Regiment
1198th SP Assault Artillery Regiment

2nd Air Army

1st Guards, 2nd Guards & 3rd Air Assault
  Corps
4th & 6th Guards Air Bomber Corps
2nd, 5th & 6th Air Fighter Corps

208th Air Night Bomber Division
98th & 193rd Guards Air Reconnaissance
  Regiment
222nd Air Transport Regiment

3rd Guards Tank Army

6th Guards Tank Corps

51st, 52nd & 53rd Guards Tank Brigades
22nd Guards Motorised Rifle Brigades

385th Guards, 1893rd & 1894th SP Assault
  Artillery Regiments
3rd Guards M/C Battalion

7th Guards Tank Corps

54th, 55th & 56th Guards Tank Brigades
23rd Guards Motorised Rifle Brigades

384th Guards, 702nd & 1977th SP Assault
  Artillery Regiments
4th Guards M/C Battalion

9th Mechanised Corps

69th, 70th & 71st Mechanised Brigades
91st Tank Brigade
383rd Guards, 1507th & 1978th SP Assault
  Artillery Regiments
100th M/C Battalion

16th SP Assault Artillery Brigade
57th Guards & 90th Independent Tank
  Regiments
50th M/C Regiment

4th Guards Tank Army

5th & 6th Guards Mechanised Corps
10th Guards Tank Corps
68th Guards Tank Brigade
70th Guards SP Assault Artillery Brigade

13th & 119th Guards Independent Tank
  Regiments
7th Guards M/C Regiment

28th Army

20th, 38th Guards & 128th Rifle Corps

31st Army

1st Guards Cavalry Corps
152nd Tank Brigade
98th Independent Tank Regiment

368th Guards, 416th & 1976th SP Assault
  Artillery Regiments
21st, 45th, 49th & 58th Independent
  Armoured Train Battalions

Notes

Notes

Notes

Notes

Notes

Notes

Notes